UPON THESE SHORES

Edited by

Rebecca Mee

First published in Great Britain in 2000 by
POETRY NOW
Remus House,
Coltsfoot Drive,
Peterborough, PE2 9JX
Telephone (01733) 898101
Fax (01733) 313524

All Rights Reserved

Copyright Contributors 2000

HB ISBN 0 75432 461 3
SB ISBN 0 75432 462 1

FOREWORD

Although we are a nation of poets we are accused of not reading poetry, or buying poetry books. After many years of listening to the incessant gripes of poetry publishers, I can only assume that the books they publish, in general, are books that most people do not want to read.

Poetry should not be obscure, introverted, and as cryptic as a crossword puzzle: it is the poet's duty to reach out and embrace the world.

The world owes the poet nothing and we should not be expected to dig and delve into a rambling discourse searching for some inner meaning.

The reason we write poetry (and almost all of us do) is because we want to communicate: an ideal; an idea; or a specific feeling. Poetry is as essential in communication, as a letter; a radio; a telephone, and the main criterion for selecting the poems in this anthology is very simple: they communicate.

CONTENTS

Live Music - The Spanish Bar, Kinsale, Ireland	Patricia Hopkins	1
The Riches Of Life	Margaret Gleeson Spanos	2
We Are The Children From This War	A Houghton	3
Mother's Lament	Margaret Boddy	4
Portrait Of Me	Joan E Blissett	6
The Way We Were	Paul A Reeves	7
Seven Years Old In Fifty-One	David O'Regan	8
How The Town Has Changed	Doreen Pickett	9
The Caterpillar And Mrs Paul	Sheila Rabbetts	10
Diana Queen Of Hearts (The Funeral)	Elaine Dean	11
The Walk	Anne Sackey	12
Teddy Bears	Joyce Hammond	13
Twentieth Century Muse	M McCoy	14
Who Made Me As I Am - A Toast	Janette Valentine	16
'Tizer' Women	Jackie M Creek	17
Open Doors	Cynthia Smith	18
Our Fruits Of Autumn	Bee Wickens	19
Once A Child . . .	Ian Garsine	20
Untitled	Maria Waters	21
Fishing	Sylvia Rouse	22
The Homeless	Adam Deas	24
The Way We Are	Julian Collins	25
That's Life	Harriett Turner	26
A Pottery Wench Am I	Peggy Lowndes	27
Headless Chickens	Carol Pearce Morris	28
A Sunny March Day	A J Spencer	29
The Human Kind	Daisy Ellen Jones	30
Treasured Memories	Elizabeth Myra Crellin	31
Sticky Fingers	M A Challis	32
Mountain Ash 1880	Jackie Bilton	33
For A Shilling	Anne Marie Birley	34
Remembering The Past	Sonia Bowan	35

Saturday Morning Pictures	Kris Holman	36
Winter's Fun In 1945	Rose Rawlings	37
The Chair	T A Williams	38
The Gorilla	Rosina Winiarski	39
Plus Ca Change!	Andrew A Duncan	40
Going Back In Time	Anita M Slattery	41
Farming Memories	Tessa Dewhurst	42
Memories	Gillian Mullett	44
Family Outing	Vivienne Brocklehurst	45
Boxes Of Life	Oracle	46
Old England	A F Mace	48
Mission In Life	Jamie Barnes	49
My Ex . . .	Naomi Elisa Price	50
Small Shop Windows	M Courtney Soper	51
Chapels Shrines Churches Gone	Paul Faulkner	52
Duffy's Pick-Up	Andria Cooke	54
The Evacuee	Brenda M Hadley	55
Recollections	Mary Cane	56
Remember?	Peggy L Haynes	57
Echoes	Pat Marsh	58
Scattered	G White	60
Family	Sheila Waller	61
Washing Day	O Carey	62
Childhood Memory (A Field Of Poppies)	Hannah Yates	63
Distant Memories	Tilla B Smith	64
Summer Memories	Judy Thomas	65
Mirage Of Memory	Rachael Shipston	66
Manchester Mime	Pat Mitchell	67
Avenues	Mel Leggett	68
Love's Final Episode	Kenny Morrison	69
The Necessity Of Nostalgia	Denis Martindale	70
First Impressions	Ray Ford	71
On The Beach	Rebecca Bennett	72
Memories	M Mandell-Lynn	73
Farewell To My Best Friend Vera	Esther Hawkins	74

The Way We Were	M E Smith	75
Young Love	Margaret C Rae	76
Rock Star	Ann Bryce	77
Cornish Magic	Ann Linney	78
Dream Upon A Star	L Booth	79
Long Ago	G Poole	80
Russian Culture In 1984	Christina B Cox	81
Thoughts	Carol Williams	82
Cousins From America	Joy Cooke	83
If You Were Really . . .	Fiona E Pearce	84
First Impressions Of Provence	Tony Matts	85
Worlds Apart Within	Terry Baldwin	86
The Eyes Of An Iban Chief	J C McKenzie	87
Japan	Kathryn Seymour	88
Sunrise	Susan Barnes	89
Blackpool 2000	Irene Munro	90
The Train	Jamie Barnes	91
Far And Away	S Esat	92
First Love	Deborah L Wilson	93
Down Under	Anne Greenhow	94
My Favourite Place	Fiona Ball	95
Delays	G T D Skelton	96
A Proper Holiday At Last	Linda Webster	98
Natural Beauty	Sheila Waller	99
The Apple Orchard	Pat Heppel	100
Oberammergau	Sheila Wyatt	102
June In Argyll	Elinor Wilson	103
The Hunger Of The Heart	Joan Hands	104
N'Djamena	Katherine Holmstrom	105
The Mission	Ernest L Hannam	106
Ronnie's Life On The Oil Rig	Olive Peck	107
May 1997 - Scottish HIghlands	Irene G Corbett	108
Memories!	R Hogg	109
The International Eisteddfod	Joyce M Turner	110
Echoes Of Africa	Handsen Chikowore	111
John Muir Wood	Lesley Anne Stevenson	112
Taj Mahal	J M Harvey	113

Live Music - The Spanish Bar, Kinsale, Ireland

Anticipation.
Nine-thirty - no sign of the players;
The noisy minutes drag in a quartet of silence.
A round table - four chairs ready.

Nine-fifty - they appear in the doorway.
The Guinness creeps willing, yet slow, into the glasses.
Seated they are pensive.
A raised eyebrow; a nod; a knowing look.
A long draught for the soul's inspiration.
A single fiddle sings out the embryo of an idea;
Communicated, understood and developed,
Wedded in harmony, the melody is born.

This she knows; this she heard in the womb;
Rocked in her mother's body,
Who knew it from her mother before her.
She stands in the crowded bar,
In a genetic awakening.
Steps she knows in her head
She dances in her mind, where there is space.
Her hands tap out the rhythm
On the round drum of her belly
For the new life that is in her womb.

Patricia Hopkins

The Riches Of Life

We were carefree, we were glad and ran barefoot on the land,
We ran naked in the sun, good food came from the land.
Parents worked very hard, making butter, bread and jam.
Current buns, apple tart, gooseberries and the rhubarb made
The juices flow.
We were sure that we were poor as we wore hand me downs.
It's older now I be, to find that we had riches to our hands,
Even better in our heads and in our hearts.
Sometimes now when I do think, wartime in a city must
have been some hell.
No great complexes from those hand me downs, I just love
To browse around the charity shops, sport the best dress in
Town.
I am grateful for what was the fashion then, when we were
Kids.
Caring for each other was 'The in thing then'.

Margaret Gleeson Spanos

WE ARE THE CHILDREN FROM THIS WAR

We are the children from this war
We can only tell you what we heard
and the things we saw.
They killed our mothers, fathers too
and those who are very young will
never really know.
They will only have the memories of the
bombs when they exploded, always they will
remember the big bangs they heard as noise,
and those of them who are older and this
they will never forget.
For they won't know what it's like to grow up
with a family. And maybe one day himself
a wife. So, oh please God help these children
to build a good life.

A Houghton

MOTHER'S LAMENT

(Killed in Action. Thomas Kitchingman. 9.3.45)

Who will remember you when I am dead and gone?
You'll be another lost soul, lost past all remembrance.
A thing gone, never to be seen again, never to be considered.

I'll remember you. I'll garland you in roses,
You'll be festooned with warmth and love,
Gathered up, a light, a stream, an essence of pure joy.

A cherished unremitting star, a cluster of pure light.
I'll cherish you with thoughts as pure as snow
And hear your heartbeat all my life long days.

Death shall have no rule here. I'll gather you up each morning,
Share you with the sun. You'll be my balm, a comforter,
A constant manifestation of our loves and joys.

No one will take you from me, even the Gods know that's unfair.
They're willing that I should share you, I've said my prayers
And paid due respect to my duties and sacred obligations.

I need some God to know it. I'll plum the depths and search the skies
Scream and tear asunder the thick robes of night that divide us
I'll steal the time, my fingers shall rewind the clock for all of us.

I'll make contact for your brief return, a return of your life for all to see
And seeing, you'll be transubstantiated to everyone's dead soul,
Not a lost soul but found a place again among the living.

We'll have a ball, where all are invited, all our dead souls will be reunited.
You'll see your Clarence, George, Charlotte, Charles and Willy,
They'll sup with us, we'll fill our cup to overflowing.
We'll dance the time away.

And there you'll be, everyone's darling. No sinews, no bones, just you.
A dancing light of sheer exuberance.
My sweetest boy, my heart's delight.
Mother of God, why did you take him from me?

Margaret Boddy

Portrait Of Me

Our youth has gone but it appears that as we move on through
the years
I see you as you were and now. And what's it matter anyhow?
Things then were as they used to be. Is this now how you see me?
A picture not of youth and dreams. I may be one of life's has-beens
But far better to have lived and been, than lived and never to have
been,
Never dreamed, never been, never seen. Never loved, never lived,
never evergreen!
Music's sung and music's made. We remember some, some we
downgrade.
Only the fickle push aside the things they've loved. They try to hide
Or discard the finer things gone before. Fashion dictates!
They're never sure!
When modern moods are scrapped and gone, the finer classics still
live on.
Remembered for their worth. The things I've loved, I'll always love.
I loved them then, I love them now, and time is just the same
somehow.
What went before was my life made. The things I did, the things I
said
mean as much now that I am old. The things once held I still will hold.
Life's pawns can come, life's pawns can go and do what they are told
to do.
If modern shows me something good I'll keep and add it to my classic
collection,
I'll peep and from time to time select and play the good from today
and yesterday.
Now given the facts of how I feel, does this make my life more real?
Do you see me as I used to be or just the present portrait of me?
There's past, there's present, there's future. Maybe like me you can see
all three.

Joan E Blissett

THE WAY WE WERE

Lunch. First touch as you handed me the change.
You looked at me, cool as condensation,
Cold as condescension. Other lunches
Followed, each one accompanied by more
Than one excuse, but never proper cause
For your coldness. I would not tread on toes,
As you seemed to want. 'They were only friends',
You used to say, but I heard different.
Many used to come to feast on our
Misfortune, to gloat that age *was* a bar,
After all. You said that you did not mind,
But you were only marking time - again,
Keeping up appearances, until one
Who was new would come along, a fresh form
Of the old torture. When the moment came,
As sudden as it was expected, I
Soared, no longer bored by your pretence,
The cold grey light of dawn was my sunrise
Following clammy nights of your superb
Deceit.

Paul A Reeves

Seven Years Old In Fifty-One

Up the pub steps, peep into the bar
don't go any further, that's a step much too far.
Kids weren't allowed in pubs then although,
me mam did the cleaning so sometimes I'd go
round the partition and sit very still
with old Harry the blacksmith, we'd play tip-it until
Mrs Miller said 'Paddy, it's time David went home.'
and off up the lane I'd go all alone
with a bottle of Guinness, five Woodbines and crisps
to me mam who was waiting like a 'will-o-the-wisp'
beside the front gate, not worried - and yet
some words would be said much later I'd bet . . .
'What about you Paddy, keeping the boy out this late'
'Wasn't I talking to farmer Smith-Burnham and Kate
about hoeing sugar beet and later maybe
there'd be potatoes to pick and they'd think well of me
if I'd find time to look at one of their cows
and give my opinion since I know just how,
having once had a small farm below there in Cork.
Now why are you blatherin', sure can't the child walk
two hundred yards back home on his own.'
While I lay under overcoats in bed all alone
but I know that they loved me and they're arguing still
above there in heaven and waiting until
I'm up there to join them and then we'll have laughs
with Harry the blacksmith playing tip-it and draughts.

David O'Regan

How The Town Has Changed

Where has it all gone, the old town of ours
Where, as a child, I walked round for hours.
When Tyrers then stood on Liverpool Road
And Sheet Works stood up where the 'Hotties' then flowed.
When the bus terminal could be found in Bridge Street
And the Rivoli cinema had a 'double' back seat.
Where there were two markets, one covered, one not
And the old co-op cafe served a lovely hot-pot.
The Savoy and the Riv' - the Hipp' and the Cap'
Today, no more cinemas can be found on the map.
So much of St Helens has changed now for me
But it's nice to remember how it used to be.

Doreen Pickett

THE CATERPILLAR AND MRS PAUL

That was a sublime Spring
when overhead
buzz bombs and mortars
tore the Echo offices apart and
the news was told in the solemn lines of the dead.

Sis' and I leapt onto the top of our Anderson shelter
drunk with the noise.
We jigged and danced about under that terrible display.
'You little demons. You'll be the death of us all.'
Dad roared and shook his fist.

Inside was a womb of concrete and smells.
Along a sill of saw-edged stone we traced our fingers delicately,
it could split a child's skin to the bone.
We put indignant woodlice in Woodbine packets
until I trod on uncle Tike's head and laughed.

Once we took our Sunday dinner down there
while from above V2s dropped their death hush
and Dad spilled his gravy down his trousers.
Because of that we weren't allowed pudding
and Mrs Paul found a caterpillar in her knicker leg.

Later, much later we discovered the shelter
covered with corrugated tin, bramble and nettle.
We crept inside, wanting the war back again
and looked down hopefully.
But just a frog looked up at us.

Sheila Rabbetts

DIANA QUEEN OF HEARTS (THE FUNERAL)

Diana Queen of English hearts we mourn for you this day,
Our nation reels from shock and grief because you've gone away.
'Why her? So young,' we cry in pain 'Oh, what a tragic waste,
How can such vibrant beauty, be snuffed out in such haste?'
You seemed just on the threshold too of finding love at last.
A long deserved new happiness, and freedom from your past!
It's so unfair, we'll miss you so, for all the good you did,
Like stooping low and lifting high, the lonely down-trod kid!
For helping those less fortunate, identifying with pain,
For treating folk with dignity, no matter what their name.
Shunning regal protocol, you reached out to the poor,
The young, the old, the needy, to give's what you lived for!
We'll miss your beauty, poise and charm, that cheered where ere you went,
You were a princess *royal* indeed, a gift from heaven sent.
Turning now our thoughts to God, we ask His help this day;
'Be with us Lord, to light our gloom, please comfort us we pray.'
So goodbye, England's sweetest rose, the peoples own princess,
We never will forget you Di, goodnight my love, God bless.

Elaine Dean

THE WALK

Walking down the country lane.
Dog by my side, hope it doesn't rain.
Let off her lead to snuffle the hedgerow.
Cornfield changing as it starts to grow.
We cross the field, the rabbits scurry.
When people are around they're always in a hurry.
Sheep grazing in a field nearby.
Dog under control as I cross over the sty.
At the river she goes in for a dip.
I cross carefully as I don't want to trip.
The spring water oozes out of the hill.
Stop for a drink, so clear with a refreshing chill.
It meanders down to meet the main stream.
Watercress abundant, a gourmet's dream.
Towards the old railway line then head for home.
The walk is so rewarding you never feel alone.
Something different each time you go for a walk.
Mushroom pickers have visited, you can spot the odd stalk.
A variety of flowers all in bloom.
New plants growing, as there's plenty of room.
Turn back to the village, walk nearly done.
Delight in wonders I've seen under the sun.
Thoughts held forever in one's mind.
Lucky indeed, as such pleasures are hard to find.

Anne Sackey

TEDDY BEARS

Most of us when children loved our teddy bear,
Couldn't get off to sleep unless he was there.
Telling him your secrets and your hopes and dreams,
Giving him lots of loving cuddles and hugs which nearly
burst his seams.
Children love their teddies which we know is true
And even when they're grown up still have them too.
Our lovely childhood friend we cannot bear to part
So stay with me and keep within my heart.
There are some famous teddy's, Pooh, Rupert and Paddington Bear,
And some of them look tatty from all their loving care.
Some make funny noises, some of them have a squeak,
I bet you wished at sometime that your teddy could speak.
Some of them are different colours, brown or gold or blue,
But all of them are special and mean a lot to you.

Joyce Hammond

TWENTIETH CENTURY MUSE

When I was born,
There were poppies and pimpernels amidst the corn,
Dormice, corncrakes and skylarks flourished,
Horses tilled the fields, offspring to be nourished.
Milk came home in churn, ladled into a jug;
Butter cut from a tub shaped mould; the counter cat to hug.
Bacon, salted, hand sliced, thick, on a block.
Loose cash on the counter, no need for a lock.
Various children's sweets, temptingly displayed;
Chocolate dragees, coconut chips and aniseed balls filled the trays.

When I was at school there were regulations severe;
Performed by male Heads, and many spinsters sincere.
With limited training and vaulted dedication,
Unregulated punishments, giving sadistic gratification.
Truanting brought the Board Officer to the door:
Juvenile courts decided if the parents' needs were more,
For farm labouring, family caring or extra money,
To feed their ever growing families with milk and honey.

When I went to work there were plenty of jobs,
Whilst war number two, Britain's youth it robs.
With no Welfare State women needed support
Little food, cigarettes, clothing coupons, and no fruit to import.
No street lights or car head-lamps; house windows blacked at night,
No Health Service for unplanned pregnancies, before the men took flight.
Little oil for transport or coal to keep us warm.
Air raids destroying buildings; terror replacing calm.
For me, a naive teenager, during these dangerous years,
It gave excitement, happiness, maturity, interspersed with fears.

When I got married there was nowhere to live;
The bombs had levelled cities and no shelter could they give.
Two rooms were ours, in a house we shared with seven more,
In a Liverpool suburb not far from the shore.
No money for a family, no contraceptive pill,
Husband a mature student, with eighteen months study still.
No longer dreams of a car, house and garden,
Love learns to survive amid frustrations to pardon.

And now I am old, there are fantastic inventions;
Satellites in the sky, with lasers and space stations.
Supersonic flight and hydro-foil travel,
Computers, world wide web and internet to unravel.
Microwaves, cloning and gene modification,
C.J.D. new variant, Ecstasy and Viagra titillation.
Babies grown in test-tubes, body parts to exchange,
At the start of a new millennium, what next in the scientists range?

M McCoy

WHO MADE ME AS I AM - A TOAST

And here's a toast to those who loved
And nurtured me from birth,
To those who schooled and tutored me
And helped me know my worth.

And here's to those in friendship, who
Brought warmth and fun to me,
And in the sharing of their tears
Bestowed humility.

And here's a toast to Judas, whom
My faith did truly test,
And helped me to respect and love
The measure of the rest.

Janette Valentine

'TIZER' WOMEN

Mothers, daughters, sisters, aunts,
With turbaned heads - crowns of their class,
Spew through the factory gates at close of shift.
Shoulders slumped from years of toil,
And crossed forearms like mutton legs
Held tight against their heaving chests,
Their red raw hands shoved in armpits.

Leather aprons stained and wet
Bound around their hefty thighs,
Buxom girths sway with each stride,
And steel-capped clogs spark every flag.
Haggard, hardened, old before time -
Skin the colour of the grimy brick streets,
Heavy-eyed they head for home . . .

And more demands, so few rewards,
For labours passed, without a voice,
This is their lot, where one can but hope
- For a jug of 'mild' on Fridays,
And a packet of 'Woody's'.

Jackie M Creek

Open Doors

In the dim and distant thirties, we kept an open door.
Neighbours all were welcome, and we had friends galore.
Kids skated up the roadways; adventured in the park;
    Camped around the countryside, and played out after dark.

In war we offered shelter when bombs disturbed our dreams.
For one whole year our little house was bulging at the seams!
Danger drew us closer; we cared and shared as one.
    (Nowadays we wonder, where's that camaraderie gone!)

We have locks and shrill alarms on the home and car;
Cameras track your move, no matter where you are.
Strangers can't be friends, we warn our little daughter.
    Don't take sweets, they could be drugged, is what we've taught her.

Yet mem'ries of those bygone days forever will remain.
Most of all the friendly trust, we must somehow regain.
So how do we recapture that caring neighbourhood?
        By doing unto everyone, only what is good.

Cynthia Smith

Our Fruits Of Autumn

I remember when leaves were green on the tree,
And flowers smiled sweetly on you and on me;
We danced and we sang, and played in the hay;
The sun shone down brightly and warmed our day,
For then was our springtime with summer to follow
When, in life's pleasures, we freely could wallow.

As summer wore on, sometimes 'twas cool;
The sun hid its rays and then, as a rule,
The storm clouds would gather and raindrops did fall,
Bringing us tears, beyond recall.
Trees lost their flowers, leaves changed their bright hue,
And life bore its troubles for me and for you.

Now autumn is with us and harvest is near;
We'll gather the fruits of that we hold dear,
For life is more mellow for me and for you,
And we can look back now on our seasons anew.
The leaves on the trees are gold, red and green;
Flowers are gone, but their fruits can be seen . . .

So, is not this season the most beautiful time,
Fulfilling and mellow, when all is in rhyme;
Coming together in glorious attune,
A hymn to our seasons, - our suns and our moon?
Our fullness of life, and all we've attained
Together, our love, duly acclaimed.

Bee Wickens

Once A Child . . .

Blow me a tune on your cornet
Mr Ice cream man.
You and your 99 angels
In your wafer-thin van.
Take me to heaven on a rocket,
A lolly-ice that's the best.
Show us your favourite flavours
In a chocolate tea-leaf vest.
You are the friend of kiddies,
You keep our hopes alive.
Serve me before these children -
I'm nearly sixty-five.

Ian Garsine

UNTITLED

Where were you when he got shot?
Standing in the park
And at the new Millennium?
Standing in the dark
Where were you when he got in?
The minister of the age
Standing on my own in rage
Where were you when the small man won?
The corporation came out tops?
And where were you when the world stood still?
Standing in the flock.

Maria Waters

FISHING

(October to December - Sunday mornings - English and Scottish Drifters sail from Lowestoft.)

Boats sail out to sea one by one,
The 'Herring Fishing' has begun.

A crowd gathers at the Pier Head,
Boats sound their horn; full steam ahead.

Who is first to reach the fishing ground,
Hoping shoals of herring can be found.

The Dogger Bank is a favourite spot,
And luck plays a vital part.

Nets are cast into the sea,
Crew then take a break for tea.

A welcome breeze stirs herrings up,
Silver fins swim near the top.

Later, echoes the Mate's call,
'All hands on deck, it's time to haul!'

Eager fishermen pull nets aboard,
Soon fish are piled high in the hold.

Bows low in the water with this load,
Time to sail . . . Homeward.

Deckies land herrings on the quay,
Wondering what price a cran will be.

Noisy gulls gather and circle,
Swoop to snatch a tasty morsel.

Next crew wait for the high tide,
Releasing the ropes from the side.

The boat is then turned around,
To sail again for the fishing ground.

For years fishermen earned a living from the North Sea
Now the 'Home Fishing' is history.

Sylvia Rouse

The Homeless

When I walk down the long narrow street,
I see some kids searching for something to eat,
They pick up food, off the floor,
Then go in search for something more,
When they turn the narrow bend,
To people they ask, may you lend,
Most of these people are poor and homeless,
These are the people on which we should focus,
We should give some stuff to the poor,
And try to help them a little more,
They need food just like we do,
So please make donations to
Raise some money, to them you give,
So they can buy some food to live.

Adam Deas (11)

THE WAY WE ARE

Let's live upon this time my love,
that one day we can look back to
the way we were, the clothes we wore,
the model of the motor car,
the passion in a shooting star.
and how our city lay before
our bedroom window, looking out
upon the local life we knew.

So let our love and joy shine through
all troubles that we come unto
so once upon a time, one day,
with hands upon our hearts we'll say
we're glad we lived our lives that way.

Julian Collins

THAT'S LIFE

Those long gone days when times were hard,
Were fought through to the end.
I struggled through the good and bad,
It drove me round the bend!

Though now my family have all grown,
And life has sailed through fine.
They now have children of their own,
So you'd think I'd have more time!

But no, it's 'Nana, can I have?'
Or 'Can we come to you?'
There's just no peace, even in the lav!
But I just sail on through . . .

I look upon their dirty face,
And count right up to ten.
I grab the soap . . . Then start to pace . . .
Oh . . . Here we go again!

Harriett Turner

A Pottery Wench Am I

Although it seems like yesterday
My early life is far away.
But I know I will always say
A Pottery Wench am I!

My family were true Pottery folk.
A terraced house was home.
A narrow street, a factory wall.
My eyes still see it, dark and tall.

But in that street, 'twas safe to play.
Few cars came by to spoil our day.
We played our games till it was dark.
The street was our own leisure park.

The back of these small houses
Looked across at Shelton Bar.
The steelworks nightly firework show.
So bright it made our faces glow.

The war just past, times were hard.
Dad made a garden in the yard.
To feed his family was his aim.
An expert gardener he became.

Although the street was dark and drab.
We made the best of what we had.
Two caring parents made us see
How bright a place of love can be.

Though many years have slipped away
And life is different from those days.
But if I'm asked, I proudly cry
A Pottery Wench am I!

Peggy Lowndes

HEADLESS CHICKENS

With dinner in mind, my grandpa is told
To kill a plump chicken - 'Please, nothing too old.'
My brother and I follow close in this tracks,
Watching enthralled as he sharpens his axe.
He seeks an apt victim from in the hen run,
The scrawniest bird is the singled-out one.
With the rest of the flock in a state of shell-shock,
We follow them closely back to the block.
A swift glint on blade, the head's on the ground -
Is it a dream that it headless ran round?
Our mother's convinced that to see such a sight
Will bring us both nightmares with screams of deep fright,
But this did not happen, we made it a game,
'Killing a Chicken' then promptly became
A favourite pastime, by chopping the 'head'
Off a large paw-paw leaf, while shouting 'You're dead!'

Now forty years on with two pigs to rear,
I'm overcome with my mother's fear.
They're taken to slaughter, remorse is too late,
There's pork in the freezer and chops on the plate.

I'm asked, 'Is this pork? Is this Pinky or Perky?'
In cowardice I shout, 'No, you're wrong! This is turkey!'

Carol Pearce Morris

A Sunny March Day

I remember a primrose bank,
A primrose bank on a sunny March day.
The soft and feathery new spring grass,
White clouds that sailed on a deep blue sea,
Dreaming dreams as they drifted past,
Holding hands, my Johnny and me.

The noisy rooks in the tall elm trees,
Like rackety lads on a building site,
Each twig flown in for his love to please,
Sweet eighteen and the world was bright.

Gazing out at the drizzling rain,
Watching the drops as they glint and dance,
And then I'm back in the grass again,
Remembering youth and a sweet romance,
Oh yes I remember a primrose bank.
A primrose bank on a sunny March day.

A J Spencer

The Human Kind

When I was young, I had a grandma.
She wore a bonnet and a shawl,
She wore on her feet lace up boots,
Well that's what I recall.

I never thought I would grow old,
Like my grandma seemed to me,
The old ones came from another world,
Young, they could never have been.

Now I am old, and the young ones know
Little of my world,
We wrote with a pen, with the words in
Our heads
Not on a computer screen -
The kinds of tasks we had to do, the young
Have never seen.

But I could not solve the problems
The young have today -
From horses and carts to aeroplanes,
And rockets to the moon,
We have come a long long way.

And it seems to me that very soon
Machines of every kind will fill our
Buildings and our minds,
The young will no longer know
The world of the human kind.

Daisy Ellen Jones

TREASURED MEMORIES

Three little girls very first day at school.
To appear late would have been against
the rule.

'Oh! Mama' we cried.
'We are big girls to go in a pram'
But thinking about it, it was more
Like a tram.
There we were.
Three little girls crouched low.
As we swayed back and fro.
We hoped against hope, we couldn't,
Possibly be seen.
To us it was like a tormented dream.
But Mama always used her brain and common sense.
To get us there on time was of course her intent
Of our feelings Mama always thought.
And the pram was quietly brought
To a halt out of sight of the school court.
So nobody was any the wiser about our four
Wheeled transport.
I must underline we arrived on time.
And I am pleased to share this memory in rhyme.

Being triplets we had a wonderful childhood, and
We enjoyed each other's company, immensely.
Going to bed was a pleasure, we quietly chatted
And Elaine was the storyteller.
Dorothea and I nudged her if she started to
Nod off 'Tell us more, don't go to sleep.'
I remember there was much fun and laughter.
And we were so lucky to have such loving, sensible
Parents, and older sisters.

Elizabeth Myra Crellin

Sticky Fingers

Real sweets came from jars,
stored on wooden shelves.
They were all stuck together,
we had to separate them ourselves.
Weighed on the scales, packed in white bags,
a treat for a small child's eyes.
The modern day plastic packaging,
takes away the surprise.
Sherbet drops, wine gums, fruit drops,
everybody's mixtures, just to name a few.
As children these were friendly names,
all our friends always knew.
Sweets never taste the same now,
and yet they are much dearer in price.
When we were growing up, as children,
sweets tasted sticky and nice.

M A Challis

MOUNTAIN ASH. 1880

After walking forever they appear,
The ghosts.
Against the blackness of the sky.
Old silhouettes.
Haunched, holding tin boxes.
Rats are hungry, ready to gorge on meagre sandwiches.
Old cloth caps pulled down against the night snow.
Scarves, worn jackets and waistcoats.
The cage pulls too like the crack of a whip.
Stinging.
The descent begins under the mountain.
Nothing's said.
The damp air hits like a repugnant lover.
The walk to the seam, miles, in black oily water to the knees,
A weathered hand reaches for comfort on timber supporting the roof,
As that of the breast of his woman.
Legs as tired as a thousand years trudge along narrow rails.
Down, down into the belly of the woman calling.
Each shovelful of the black jewel thrown upwards.
Old stockings and pants taking the strain of kneeling and dragging
Along the ground.
Sips of water replacing the salty sweat.
The sweet black coal shining in water, glistening, beckoning.
The whiteness of eyes, staring, searching, proud and afraid.
The long walk upwards harder than the descent.
Screaming limbs and breaking hearts.
Desperate for that first sweet gulp of air.
Replenished only by the thought of the warm flesh
That will be lying by him in his bed.
The long walk home.
And the sad knowledge of returning tomorrow.

Jackie Bilton

For A Shilling

She met a man when she was young, who loved her for a shilling,
He bet a friend he would bed her, for he thought she would be willing.
The bet was won, her life was lost, to years of strife and labour,
For love was lost and life was such a bitter pill to savour.
Her children born of love forsworn, if only for a shilling.
They were the greatest love she had, and for them she was willing.
Worth to her the gold on earth, much more than but a shilling.
Then love was lost at what a cost, a lot more than a shilling.
Life, sometime good, sometime bad, sometime right down-hearted,
Until it was so bad for them, that for the best they parted.

She met a man from northern climes, with him she felt much safer,
But after years she lived and learned, he had a selfish nature -
They parted then, and once again she sort to love another,
They are as one all said and done, with her his love he covers.
So for today together they have love for one another,
With hopes that neither one of them, a new love will discover.
From time to time she thinks of then, when she was young, beguiling,
For that was when her life was worth a tiny silver shilling.

Anne Marie Birley

REMEMBERING THE PAST

As I was standing under the tree
A little thought came over me
Thoughts of joyful playful scenes
That took me back to a childhood game
Thoughtlessness, no time for sorrow
Pain I did not know that name
For the playing fields was my remote space
How I wish I could go back to them
And start my life all over again
There are so many things I would push aside
I would not even let them guide
My life would be oh so different now
But it is not too late to go back again
Pick up the pieces and move forward
For only death can change that game
So Lord strengthen me and give me time
To mend my ways and smoothen my heart.

Sonia Bowan

SATURDAY MORNING PICTURES

Sat'day morning, down the Regal, opp'site Woolwich Town 'all.
Franky, David, me and Andy. Daryl came an'all.
Down the common, past the barracks, sentry in 'is box,
In front of empty p'rade ground, underneath the clock.

Franky's got a Woodbine, nicked it from 'is dad.
'Pass it on Dave, Daryl's turn.' 'No, Mummy says it's bad.'

Franky's got an idea, 'e pays, goes in, let's us in round the back.
That way we save some money to spend on sweets an' that.
Daryl says 'It's stealing,' says 'e'll tell 'is mum.
Andy says 'e'd better not, and kicks 'im up the bum.

Goofy, Bugs Bunny, Donald Duck,
Followed by a cowboy, with a bit of luck.

'We like to laugh and have our sing song,
Just a happy crowd we are,
We're all pals together,
We're minors of the ABC.'

Down to pie an' eel shop, wait for 192,
Watch 'em slither in their box, 'til someone goes in to
Take some eel home for their tea.
Wriggle, wriggle, slit, chop chop. Don't seem fair to me.

And then came Daryl's mum knocking at my door.
Told Ma I smoked, told Ma I swore,
Told Ma I sneaked in the back door.

Can't go to pictures any more.

Kris Holman

WINTER'S FUN IN 1945

It was a cold frosty day
The canal was covered with ice
We children used to roam
Not to heed Mother's advice.
Treading carefully, step by step
Would the ice take our weight?
Along came this big man
Showing us how he could skate.
The figure of eight we had to watch
And his waltzing was full of pride
But we did enjoy ourselves
Though we could only slide.
He went up and down the canal
With his hands behind his back
Till he went near the bridge
On thin ice, and suddenly, crack.
We children saw the danger,
Went sliding to the bank
Climbed up on the towpath
Watching as he sank.
Good job it is not deep
We laughed and joked
He crawled out to our applause
Pride all gone and soaked,
So off we all went
Home to get our tea.
Lesson learnt, never show off,
It could easy happen to me.

Rose Rawlings

THE CHAIR

The chair/ligneous.
Your presence of vicarious impetus,
still the impression of your body sits permeated.
The warmth of your breath
brushes my ears,
your smell still drifts
in clouds of scent,
to enhance the drifting mind.
Your voice escapes from objects,
echoes,
imprisoned in the still air,
unmoved from past to present.

T A Williams

THE GORILLA

One day in the 'forties
A little girl was taken to the zoo.
She saw lots of animals, had a ride
And visited the birds and reptiles too.

They had a picnic lunch
And bought some souvenirs,
But when they went to the primates
The little girl was close to tears.

There, huddled at the back of his cage
Was a solitary ape.
He stared ahead as though unaware
Of the jostling crowds which came to gape.

Some boys tried to goad him with grimaces,
But he was immune to such routing torment.
'Oh, the poor thing, how cruel,' somebody said,
'To be confined to lifelong imprisonment.'

The little girl read all the details
Which were on a plaque outside the cage,
She realised that the gorilla was very old
And felt a growing sense of outrage.

He sat motionless and dark against the straw,
A magnificent creature of awesome size,
But what impressed her was his gentle face
And the sad expression in his eyes.

When she got home that night
She was asked if she had enjoyed her treat.
'Well, I liked some of it,' she said.
'The baby animals were really sweet.'
Then she thought of the gorilla and knew what she would do.
'If I became queen for a day I would banish every zoo.'

Rosina Winiarski

Plus Ca Change!

The excitement, the challenge and censure
we knew in the days of our youth
were like wine in those days of adventure
before we guessed at the truth.
There was nothing we could not achieve
irrespective of how off-beat it was;
we laughed at the risks, alive in our hearts
no matter how 'celebre' the cause.
And life as it was, thus continued
until the feminine voice, quietly heard -
no longer the sense of adventure,
we're docile like 'coos in the herd'!
The weemen are nou the braw leaders
and handle the purse strings an aa
an we men are the hewers and diggers
an do as we're telt - it's the law!

Andrew A Duncan

GOING BACK IN TIME

I am going back in time,
We kids watched the trains,
Backwards and forwards they came,
Being driven by coal, with lots of steam,
For many years, now this is not seen:

All the kids played in the street,
After school we would meet,
On the pavements, playing hop scotch,
From that, lots of fun we got:

Simple years ago, the games,
And the skipping rope . . .
Memories of past days,
We who were young once,
Our playtimes, we often remember and note:

We may have wished to grow up,
Only because we wanted to leave school,
That is when responsibility comes to you,
And naught about that can we do:

You all look back on childhood times,
As with each passing hour . . .
They fade away and are gone,
That is honest, so enjoy your youth,
Because time has lots of power:

That's right you little ones,
Never wish to grow up fast,
Just wish your childhood could last.
Take a note of these words, that we once heard.

Anita M Slattery

FARMING MEMORIES

The farmer rose early at crack of dawn,
He had cows to milk both night and morn;
Milked one by one by his deft hand,
He knew the demands of life on the land.

With his yoke never easy nor burden light
He carried two pails either side upright;
The warm milk flowed into churns pristine
Inside a dairy so spotless and clean.

The friesian cows all had a name,
As pedigrees they were used to fame;
There was Monica, Cora and Judy too,
Bellina and Poppy to name but a few.

Two large brown horses Robert and Tom
Pulled a mowing machine along;
They cut the corn all ready to glean
And a handsomer pair was seldom seen.

A loveable collie who came from Gwent
Followed the farmer wherever he went;
He was more than a match for everything
Be it sheep or cows or the bull with his ring.

The farmer's wife looked after the hens
Ever free to roam and not in pens;
She fed and watered them twice a day,
Collecting the eggs that they would lay.

The daughters' pony called Bonaparte
Conveyed them to school in a governess cart;
Trotting along in the dry or the wet
Afforded a pleasure they will never forget.

The seasons rolled by then the farmer died
And those who were left just sat and cried;
His dog kept watch by the back door in vain
As he departed this life without any pain.

Some memories were happy and others sad,
One took the good as well as the bad;
Remembering those days of yesteryear
Induces both joy and sometimes a tear.

Tessa Dewhurst

MEMORIES

Among the first memories that I recall was the Saturday crush at the picture hall.
Sixpence it cost for a seat in the stalls, ninepence for sweethearts at the back by the wall.
A whole shilling was spent for a seat up the stairs, where posh folk looked down and sat with hats on in pairs.
The organ would play with an enthusiastic display, the lights all went down as the curtains swung away.
Old Mother Riley with her daughter named Kitty, Laurel and Hardy brought such joys with their ditties.
Abbot and Costello made us fit to burst, and the Three Stooges and Marx Brothers gave us such a thirst.
The lights then came up Mantovani played his strings, and then the feature, before God Save the King.
After an ice cream the theatre was all hushed as great stars of the day, exploits brought a blush.
Ginger Rogers and Fred, danced with great zeal and by the end of the film their love was sealed.
The swashbuckling hero was each young girl's crush, Errol Flynn with a sword, moustache and gentle touch.
I remember Roy Rogers and Trigger his horse, they were so fearless against the Indian force.
And when it seemed their end was in sight, the cavalry came charging and ready to fight.
The films I see now may be very good, but somehow their heroes are just made of wood.
They never can replace that special place that they hold, those stars of my childhood that will never grow old.

Gillian Mullett

FAMILY OUTING

Wednesday was early closing day.
Soon after 1pm we set off in the Armstrong Siddeley
Towards moorland where the curlew seeks its prey
Through the dale where the Derwent flows sedately
Past Matlock Bath's petrifying well and fish pond.
To Cromford where we took the Via Gellia
And saw the tufa house and Lilies Inn beyond
Past fields where pink and purple orchids flower
Round Pickory Wood corner, in view of Haddon Hall
And on to the market town of Bakewell
Where cars were few and far between, parking free for all.
Light as gossamer, luscious and sweet to smell
Was my pink candy-floss. Delicious too the cakes
Which Mum bought at the pudding pie shop.
Dad on the banks of the Wye fed ducks and drakes.
Ashford-in-the-water was our next stop.
I paddled near Sheepwash bridge,
Tried to capture the scene in water-colours,
Shared a picnic with my parents 'neath summer foliage.
When lengthening shadows welcomed back evening hours
We returned through Chatsworth Park and watched the deer
Proud stags with antlers, does and dappled fawns.
Saw pheasants in fields, Flash dam crystal clear.
Near our village grazed Jacob sheep with curly horns.
At home we arranged our flowers, washed our dishes,
Joined neighbours on the street to gossip and chat
Leaned over the bridge to watch the fishes.
From under Gregory's roof flew the first bat
At dusk a crowd of others followed.
We climbed the stairs to our tranquil abode.

Vivienne Brocklehurst

Boxes Of Life

I look at my life around me
All sitting in little boxes
We collect so many memories
As we go through our lives.

Each one has its own story
Was that when I was young?
Is that one as I grew up?
That box is when I was eighteen
So young, so free being me.

Now that one is from my twenties
The pictures there for all to see
I was happy with life and just living
Never having much sorrow, lucky me.

This box is when I married
Now, looking at life within that box
I thought I was happy, just for a time
But it was never that way.

David had this other love
I could not compete you see
I felt as I was never there
He loved that car far more than me.

It soon lead to the parting of our ways
I know, he loved in his way
But that was not enough
I wanted to be part on the other love.

My chassis was only flesh and blood
Not shiny steel with wheels that flew round.

I am not unhappy for the things that were
Oh yes, I do miss them
But time goes on
We learn to cope.

This box has my life now
Content, with my home
I do things I like to do
Write, being with my cats and birds.

Boxes of love and life
Scattered around the room
Now, I can see tomorrow will come
Happiness here for me.

Oracle

OLD ENGLAND

Pennies, shillings, half a crown,
And now we have new pence.
No feet and inches; pints and pounds.
To me it makes no sense!

Old England now has had its day.
Happy days we have no more.
Since we joined the Europeans
And let them push straight thro' the door.

Our Kings and Queens have all but gone
With grand balls and horse parade.
Factories closed and pits are shut,
A state the Iron Maiden made.

I know my memories are quite old
And modern life is far from bleak,
I can go back were I was born,
Where time stands still in Leek.

A F Mace

Mission In Life

Standing high up on a hill,
Showing your might, strength and will.

Hundreds of men aspired to create,
And now keeping watch until their fate.

Never losing hope nor chance,
A city's dream, fine in stance.

An honour seen from miles around,
Soaring high above the ground.

Sent down to take good care,
And when judging, to be true and fair.

Proud to be, looking fourth,
Shining bright, Angel of the North.

Jamie Barnes

MY EX . . .

Do you remember of back then?
When
We were once so close . . .
Our love just seemed to grow.
If you weren't with me -
I wouldn't go.
You would walk to my house
Every night
And outside my front door
I'd have on the light.
We'd listen to music
And talk
Go for walks.
Though I can never remember
What our talking was about.
We thought it would never end
You'd said you wanted me forever.
My life to love
But I couldn't give you that.
And when I knew
I couldn't look back.
So now you're simply
A memory
In my head.

Naomi Elisa Price

Small Shop Windows

Here tunics, illuminated in silence,
In the gateway, reflective, sensuous,
Have the shop spotlights on them,
Focused here and glinting here,
Luminous with electric secrets, here in silence
Away, and not close to the homes under the sky.

M Courtney Soper

CHAPELS SHRINES CHURCHES GONE

Philistines,
Canaans,
Trample the past,
Cut,
Paste,
New lies.
Unexpected,
You roll keen blades
Across legs,
Then ask for a dance.
Impossible.
Gouge eyes,
Glue tongues.
Blind.
Speechless.
Leaves only
Beer,
Shouts on the square,
Weak minds,
Chatter of ladettes,
Screams in high pitches.
Choose the mall,
Hot hoppings,
Busy,
Unprincipled television crews.
Why open again dark rooms
In a mind that were better shut
Or exchange respectful cool silences?
The East Winds blow,
Shepherds' tracks ever fainter,
Lapwing and larks gone,
The racer caught
By the hawks.

Do buzzards fly higher
Or the albatross
Still sweep the southern Oceans?
Do hearts still glow
Inside ruins and blackened cathedrals?
While here, devils make play
The chaffings of an imprisoned mind.

Paul Faulkner

Duffy's Pick-Up

We all looked on in shocked dismay,
Ponies and riders, with shamed surprise,
The day they took roan Jimmy away.

July, all brooding stillness, lay
Across the common, thick with flies,
And we looked on in shocked dismay,

To see the knacker's tall van sway,
Vile name emblazoned on its sides,
They day they took roan Jimmy away,

A piteous creature, dull blue-grey,
Led up the ramp, blank sunken eyes.
We all looked on in shocked dismay.

As darkness claimed him girls gave way
To dumb grief we could not disguise,
The day they took roan Jimmy away.

When from the closed van came a neigh,
The ponies shook us with goodbyes,
And we looked on in shocked dismay,
The day they took roan Jimmy away.

Andria Cooke

The Evacuee

She came on her birthday,
Our little wartime evacuee,
Her dad was in the navy,
Serving far out at sea.
It was a day in Nineteen Forty-four
When we heard that knock upon the door,
We invited her in and unpacked her case,
Seeing the unhappy look upon her face.
Brenda, for that was her name
Became one of the family
And we were glad that she came.
I was thirteen and she was just nine,
A borrowed sister in a year in time.
Peace arrived as the year passed on,
We said our goodbyes
And then she was gone.
Many years have passed by
And we are still in touch
Remembering the year
That meant so much.

Brenda M Hadley

RECOLLECTIONS

Memories are golden, though some laced with tears,
Stirring to life beneath layers of years;
World War - or childhood - the happy - the sad -
Losses or carefree days - good things or bad.

Who can remember? Perhaps you weren't born,
Peace from an Armistice, uniforms worn;
Poppies, remembrance: from families wrenched
Young men, such young men, at death's door entrenched.

Memories of ration books, searchlights, black streets,
Gas-masks in boxes - four ounces of sweets -
Newsreels of evil on cinema screens,
Terrible silence at foul death-camp scenes . . .

Children's Hour, wireless (the video unknown),
*Granadiers, prefabs - young Durbin's 'My Own',
Memories are guardians of green fields long gone,
Clear sea's untainted waves when the sun shone.

Memories gleam silver - the Thames running free,
Jam-jars of minnows, the bus back for tea;
Queuing for nylons, a penn'orth of chips,
Skipping ropes, mud-pies - and tops lashed by whips . . .

Memories from old days or only last week,
Faces - and voices that no longer speak;
Close your eyes, linger awhile at the gate
That memory opens: the space age can wait . . .

* 'Granadiers' was the name given to youngsters who attended Saturday matinees at the local Granada Cinema.

Mary Cane

REMEMBER?

Remember, once upon a time
Spring meant a happiness sublime,
A magic mood, an April day
A place where sorrow couldn't stay;
When we were young and life a rhyme,
Remember, once upon a time?

Remember, once upon a day
The war swept all our spring away
Leaving us hell and blood, and eyes
That looked on death, not paradise;
Bringing us sweat and toil and tears
And we grew old beyond our years,
Remember? All the laughter gone,
The kisses didn't linger on,
Tennis and dancing half the night;
The fairy castles built so bright
Were lost in fire and fear and splendour -

And I lost you, my love - remember?
1941.

Peggy L Haynes

ECHOES

Echoes of the past
Reverberate
Around the inside of my head;
Resonating,
Bouncing,
Rising to crescendo the more that they
Replay
Across the forefront of my mind.

Screams from the past
Pierce the unseen world
Behind the silence of my ears;
Assault me with intensity,
Insistently demanding to be heard.

From moments that are frozen
In the great continuum
Of time,
Pain from the past
Cries out at me
Through eyes of babes that pleaded for my help
A quarter century ago.

The bruising
And the blood I look upon
Behind the false facade I wear
Colour the stains of guilt
I still bear in my heart.

Scars from the past
Remain a source of endless pain
So brutally unforgiving
In its rawness.

The past is powerfully present,
Echoing
In the now.

Pat Marsh

SCATTERED

As a child
Life was so poor,
Poverty had struck
Behind our closed door.
For into the future
We had to proceed
Myself and three brothers
A lot we did need.
The thoughts of our parents
Would have been nice,
But up until now
We've paid the price.
Scattered around family
Is how it used to be,
'Cos outside my nan's one night
My father attempted suicide
In front of me.
Outside in his car
Is where he did sit,
Amongst the alcohol and pills
He did so spit.
I couldn't get out straight away,
As my nan would say, no,
Sooner or later he would just go.
I knew this was not right
And something was wrong,
So soon did she realise
The extent of my plea,
Now in my head lives
The memory you see.

G White

FAMILY

Brothers and sisters
Living so far away
No time to come for a day
Write soon - send some letters

I often think of the times
When we were of younger years
What fun we had together
Cared for by Father and Mother

We all had fun and games
Dressing up like kings and queens
Playing shops after fireworks day
Dancing on the 1st of May

Then we went our separate ways
Working hard to earn our pay
We have homes in other places
Lots of friends, smiling faces

Even now we have a bond
Though we are miles apart
Of each other we are still fond.

Sheila Waller

WASHING DAY

Washing day, as we old ones know,
Was always Monday, come rain, hail or snow.
Fire under a boiler, the water to heat,
Dolly tub, wringers, clogs on your feet.
Rubbing board, scrubbing brush, block of soap,
All were required with the washing to cope,
Not to mention starch, dolly blue or cream,
Now it all seems like a bad dream.
Washing day is no longer a chore,
Just press a button when you've closed the door.
One hour later the laundry is done,
Biologically clean, well rinsed and spun,
Without wet floors, or aching back,
No clothes maidens or overhead rack.
So much for 'The good old days',
There's a lot to be said for modern ways.

O Carey

Childhood Memory (A Field Of Poppies)

A red expanse
Of lace-like
Shimmering wings
Red -
Against floating puff balls
Meandering through
A 'forget-me-not-sky'.
Interspersed
With stout white daisies
With marigold centres
Inviting
Buzzy bees
And flippery butterflies . . .

Heaven in a childhood dream.

Hannah Yates

Distant Memories

Talking to a friend memories flooded back
Of a time from more than thirty-five years ago
Recalling only sunny days and sand-castles
Missionaries visiting our summer resort
A harmonium that had to be pumped to issue music to sing by
To entice all and sundry who were on the beach
Those of all ages gathered round a castle we helped build
If the wind blew seawards then boats flooded back
Children sitting, adults standing, all giving space to others
Then leaving in different directions, depending on our ages
Lovely dates on lovely afternoons
Holidaying from boarding school, those two weeks were fun.
Growing up still in my teens I didn't always visit
Being the tiresome youngest no one wanted to accompany!
At seventeen made to leave school with a year to spare
And sent to stay with friends.
Welcoming missionaries in northern Japan
Showing me the difference between their home
And my windswept, craggy land of Wales.
In Amorie thick snow blocked the garages and doors
The height darkening the windows of the wooden houses
With under-floor heating and beds rolled out to sleep
Washing ourselves in round, wooden, neck-high baths
With a seat inside to contemplate how small the world could seem
A 'phone call summoned all those recollections
When life seemed at peace and a lifetime ahead
The world to visit and compare and enjoy
Whereas now, disabled, relying on others, but still wanting to travel
Those occasions are few and far between.

Tilla B Smith

Summer Memories

A hot summer's day - I walk down memory lane,
Thinking of days when we never saw rain.
We didn't have much, my mum, dad and me,
Just plenty of fun for all to see.
We would sit in our garden, a colourful mess,
By standards today - a jungle no less.
There were foxgloves and daisies, an apple tree too,
Cats, dogs and rabbits, much like a zoo.

We were blessed with a view that looked over the sea,
I would yearn for such places - but that was just me.
I could not be a traveller, we had no family car,
And mum would say wisely - Swansea Bay is not far!
So heavily laden we would walk to the beach,
How grateful we were - it was not beyond reach.
And just for a moment, a sight to behold!
That great Mumbles train, more precious than gold.
Tizer pop and jam sandwiches half full of sand,
And then to Victoria to hear the brass band.
We didn't have much - my mum, dad and me,
Just plenty of fun for all to see.

I had lovely friends and just for a lark,
We would visit Cwmdonkin, but home before dark.
Yes, those were the days of memories dear,
Not times of wealth, just faint hope and cheer.
Now I sit on my patio drinking cool wine,
I think of that garden and tizer pop sublime!
The place was not special, not very grand,
But Mum and Dad knew that this was God's land.
We had no great riches for all to see,
Our wealth was the love - shared by Mum, Dad and me.

Judy Thomas

Mirage Of Memory

I'd really love to help you,
But your heart still bears the scars.
I'd really love to help you
But as soon as one door opens
Another door jars.
I know it's not your fault,
That you still think of him
But I couldn't take his place
You know I wouldn't fit in.
I would really love to help you,
To ease your hidden pain
But it seems that you don't want to,
Be taught how to love again.
I hold you when you cry,
And you kiss me,
Though I know
That is isn't me who you can see.
Just a mirage of memory,
That won't let go.
He was a fool, he'll soon realise.
Someday I know he'll see.
But my love burns as I look into your eyes
And I cry as I wish he were me.

Rachael Shipston

MANCHESTER MIME

Albert Square one summer Sunday
morning in grey. Rain clings
to skin and surfaces, afraid
of falling.

Banners herald Festival,
but still the Square
is bare of revellers.
Under the overcast, she crosses
the cobbles. Three men stand
by the Town Hall steps:
three suits of grey,
three hats with brims,
three open brollies
with rainbows painted round the rims.

They catch her eye. She glances
to the sky and shakes her head.
Palms up, she spreads her arms to say
no people in their colours.
They shake their heads as one. She shrugs,
and smiles, and drops her arms.
They shrug, and smile
and in a row
they doff their hats
in turn, and bow.

She waves, and carries on her way.
The sun comes out.

Pat Mitchell

AVENUES

Through our lives
There will be many avenues to take
Many that may lead us astray
While others will lead us to where we hope to be
Many doubts will be in place
But till we try and take that avenue
We will not know where it will lead
Where it will be
What will it bring
Through our lives
There will be many avenues to take
Many choices to think over
Many questions asked
The doubts will be in place
As through our lives there will be many
Avenues to take.

Mel Leggett

LOVE'S FINAL EPISODE

Tears falling freely
My mind's curtain is drawn
A dark veil and I know
It won't part with the dawn
Beside me lies the reason
Within me plays the torment

Words once lost, now racing
I sit with an arm round me
Mentally alone, the touch
Almost can't affect me
I stare at the ruins of
What was, heaven sent

The apologies begin
My ears close over, dismiss
Wanting to harm the face
Moments ago I wanted to kiss
Playing with my feelings as if
They were for rent

Tears over and I shake
Sleep won't come this night
Passing out, waking to
Realise it wasn't a dream, twilight
Only left with the pain
Wondering where the love went.

Kenny Morrison

THE NECESSITY OF NOSTALGIA

Nostalgia's such a wondrous thing, it drifts from joys to woes!
Reminding you of former friends, yet sometimes former foes!
Perhaps the years were good to you . . . or maybe they were bad.
Yet only you can tell what's true . . . and what irks you a tad!
If you've been lucky, praise the Lord, while you are still inclined!
Be thankful now, before you go! Don't leave and change your mind!

If your old memory serves you right, think back to childhood days,
Perhaps when yo-yos were around and proved the latest craze!
I bet you had a crush at school! Some lady teacher, eh?
How I longed to kiss Miss Willis! She was lovely, yeah, OK!
That was a long, long time ago! I bet she's now retired!
I wonder if she ever knew the dreams that she inspired!

Remember when you rode a bike, no hands across the bars?
Yeah! You must have crashed like I did, to wake up seeing stars!
Do you recall the Odeon, the Ritz or Hippodrome?
Did you watch the latest Batman, some cartoons, then run home?
And probably . . . there's somebody . . . you think owes you five quid!
Or it could be, you feel guilty . . . about something you did!

I recall some precious lover . . . her face but not her name . . .
And why we parted long ago . . . of course, she was to blame!
I'm now an adult, married too, with mortgage up to here!
I do my level best, you know, and treasure my career . . .
I'll be rich and famous one day! Yeah, baby! Wait and see!
You'll open up your newspapers and then you'll read of me!

Nostalgia's such a wondrous thing, but let's look forward, too!
Let's cherish all that was the past . . . and yet embrace the new!
Life's always what you make of it! That's what the wise men say!
Nostalgia's taught me such a lot . . . but most of all to pray!
Don't forget to save your money! Invest! Diversify!
Learn from mistakes but don't give up! And try, try, try, try, *try*!

Denis Martindale

First Impressions

From the cot
I saw the flares spitting at the sky
Making coloured images on the window
The quivering yellow and red
Giving the cold room a warm glow
Shadows of terrified people fleeing
Flames consuming the swimming baths

I lay with those two companions
Fear and measles
As an incendiary bomb demolished the outside loo
Liverpool was alight with gifts to store
The good news is, your home is standing
The bad news, there is no next door

We lived, cooked, slept in a small room
Lit by the fires outside
A small playroom for a family of three
We had two homes before this one
Both went crashing up to the sky
The fireman said we were lucky
I didn't know why.

Ray Ford

On The Beach

I walk alone on the sandy beach
Water splashing around my toes
Closing my eyes and thinking hard
You are there

Listen to the waves calling out your name
Which you coupled with mine
With a stick in the sand
I walk alone to a cave
Carved out by the fresh young times
A resting place for loving souls

I realise I know each crack each bump
The tiny little imperfections we both saw
I go further back and find what I've always been looking for
A Tupperware box filled with one day of fun
Not caring what anyone else thought
Just being for us

A plastic ring from a fairground
Gold and diamonds placed on my finger
I can smell the candy floss
That caught in the breeze and your hair
Ticket stubs from the open air show
A rock that is grey-blue-grey-blue-grey-blue-green

Four years since that day
Just one perfect day that flew in to my life
I smile at the memory of being anywhere with you
And yet could not be anywhere but here
But I am not alone.

Rebecca Bennett

Memories

Some memories are good
Some memories are bad
They cause me to remember now
The things we never had!

No motor cars to take us out
Street lights were very few,
Electricity in short supply
It's usefulness *so new.*

United were our families
Sharing in sorrow and in joy:
Helping us to face the world
Their knowledge did employ.

Remembering now, from long ago,
Words of wisdom acquired by me
Try making the world better for all
You'll be thanked eternally!

M Mandell-Lynn

FAREWELL TO MY BEST FRIEND VERA

(Who sadly died recently - with happy memories of our 3 years together, at RAF Cranwell 1941-44, especially as members of the WAAF Band)

Farewell my friend from bygone days,
Farewell my friend with loving ways,
Farewell my friend who made me laugh,
Farewell my *best friend* in the WAAF.

We both joined the band, and that was really fun,
We learned to play the flute, and learned to play the drum.
We wore the band regalia, plus the badge upon our arm,
On parade with buttons gleaming, we stood erect and calm.

How we enjoyed the band, and eagerly we'd wait,
For the command 'Band ready', woe betide if we were late.
Proudly we led the church parade, down Cranwell Avenue,
The service at the Station Hall, which soon came into view.

I remember clearly, the day I dropped my drum,
I watched it rolling onwards, then I commenced to run.
I finally retrieved it, and dashed back to my place,
There was no doubt at all, of the colour of my face.

When the parade was over, or was it the next day?
'Report to the Adjutant;' which I did without delay.
He said 'How did it happen? Why had I dropped my drum?'
I said - 'I am very sorry Sir, I don't know how it was done.'

Left turn, quick march No charge, that was a great relief,
I thought I would get Jankers, which would have caused me grief.
I still played in the band, and conquered the 'Paradiddle',
But how I dropped my drum, will forever be a *riddle.*

Esther Hawkins

The Way We Were

After 65 years of my life, so much has changed -
Could be better, or it could be worse!
Granny and Auntie lived next door
And the cousins slept happily on the floor!
We, as children went out to play -
And gas meters took just 1d per day.
The gas bills are more today!
Our fathers worked hard for little pay -
And Mothers baked bread and washed clothes for friends -
They had to make 'ends meet' not like today's trends!
They scrimped and saved before World War 2
Our street was like a family - no crime to borrow or lend.
Nobody bothered to lock up the back door.
Granddad played his piano and somebody sang!
Sunday's dinner was not usually a roast.
Sheep's head broth and potato cakes.
We used to look forward to tea when Granny bakes!
Rice pudding or treacle pie may be the sweet.
It was only Christmas dinner that was a treat!
On Christmas Eve Granddad would pluck the fowl -
There were feathers flying everywhere - this made Granny growl!
Life today has changed so much - there's computers, travel,
Television and the advanced technology and such!
So why? With life so much better in many ways?
Do I think of those times as the 'Good Old Days'?

M E Smith

Young Love

Sitting beneath, feeling safe.
The tree's covering giving comfort.
Passing the time pleasantly.
A young couple, much in love.
The sun is hot, the sky is blue.
They look into each others' eyes.
A kiss is shared, they lie talking.
Holding hands, together.
How sweet is young love.

Margaret C Rae

ROCK STAR

What is this hold he has on me?
Those blazing eyes like vast, magnetic orbs
Entice me, yielding, to profound delight.

In them exist the essence of his charm
And innocence; his zest for life; his beauty;
His eagerness and passion almost childlike.

Through them flash that scintillating power and creativity;
A dread determination; overwhelming confidence;
And obstinate will conceding no defeat.

From them shoot animated sparks of intense pleasure,
Vibrant, forcing to extreme
Infectious energy; performance dazzling.

With them he can clasp at will
Multitudes of souls within his hand
And draw them to himself.

Beneath them smoulder melancholy shadows
Of lost love, sad memories and fruitless quests
For fulfilment in life he never truly found.

Along the way he lost himself,
Strong yet vulnerable; simple yet so complex;
Successful yet afraid.

Just another ordinary human being
Experiencing human truths,
No lesser nor no better than another.

And yet he binds me in his spell;
Exudes a sense of magic, a charisma,
Characteristically him,
Which thrills me.

Ann Bryce

Cornish Magic

We sat on the beach in the evening sun
Content to be together at last;
On our honeymoon in this special place,
The magic of Cornwall surrounded us.

We talked and laughed and lay on the sand,
Swam in the sea and surfed in the surf.
Just us two - no cares in the world,
The magic of Cornwall caressed us.

We took her carry-cot down to the beach,
Talked in whispers whilst she was asleep,
Showed her the seagulls, the sky and the sea,
The magic of Cornwall encircled us.

We sat on the beach with the family,
Surrounded by sun-hats and buckets and spades;
We dug in the sand and built castles and moats;
The magic of Cornwall around us.

We watched as the children paddled and splashed,
Heard their screams of delight, joined in their fun.
Twice yearly holidays whilst they grew up,
The magic of Cornwall engulfed us.

Fifty years on we've all moved here to live,
We can visit the beaches whenever we want,
Can relive our memories of so long ago,
The magic of Cornwall has captured us.

Ann Linney

DREAM UPON A STAR

Of all the places I have known, one stays in my heart,
When I look into the sky, I dream upon that star.
A part of me, the places there, the colours stand apart,
The people that I left behind will always leave a scar.
An open wound of unhappiness, that I am far away,
A word I hear, a smell, a sound, it brings it back to me,
A happy cry, a tear of joy, a child I think of every day,
That far off place that in my dreams where I long to be.
I often wonder in the night, if she is still the same,
When darkness comes, I see her bright, a little pot of gold.
Shining through the sadness when I need to say her name,
Because her gentle touch is all that I have left to hold.
With sunshine bright, fields of green, bustling cities too,
The pungent fumes from a factory flue,
Aromas from a cafe on the corner, early morning dew,
They all remind me why I love you like I do.
She touched me, hurt me, made me cry,
I thought that I could never find a reason to return.
Then I think of how she made me feel, I sigh,
And watch hope disappear as the bridges burn.
I thought that I would never miss that place,
When I left her far behind,
To hide away from the human race,
But now I know that I was blind,
To think that I could walk away, and find a brand new hearth,
Across the universe, a million miles
That blue/green star, that they call Mother Earth.

L Booth

Long Ago

We wandered through the singing wood,
Anemones and celandine danced along the way,
We were so very happy,
On that gladsome sunny day,
The sky was blue and it was good
To walk together in the wood.

Then came the park, past water calm,
The white magnolia - pink tipped, it cast a spell,
We were so very happy,
By the fragrant hyacinth bell,
The sun shone down, and all was charm,
Because my love was on my arm.

Forty summers now have passed
Since the time I saw you last -
Now I have come back again
To where we met in a sunlit lane -
A butterfly is hovering there
Dancing in the timeless air -
So came my love on beauties wings -
And to my quiet heart it brings -
The ache of lost remembered things.

G Poole

Russian Culture In 1984

Our large group gathered in Sheffield's Town Square
For a cultural visit to Russia we were glad to share
Our first glimpse of Moscow we couldn't forget
But the tour had barely started yet.

Red Square was first upon our list
St Basil's and lenin's Tomb not to be missed
The Kremlin towers and wonderful golden domes
Schools, hospitals and museums we daily roamed.

War cemeteries we visited too
The eternal flame ever flickering through
The Bolshoi Ballet with 'Swan Lake' showing
And Cossack dancers spectacular toeing.

Yuri Gargarin's silver statue perched on high
At Pushkin museum the time did fly
We travelled the length of Gorky Street
Many friendly Russian comrades we did meet.

We watched the Anniversary Parade
Where many vehicles of war are displayed
Bright banners of red, flags and balloons
Thousands of people marched with the troops.

To Lennigrad we travelled next
The elaborate Hermitage Palace we were so impressed
Then overnight rail to Donesk
More visits, including a grand sporting complex.

A Coal mine tour, which was quite rare
The Hammer and Sickle flag was flying there
On fields and land, the women worked by hand
They had so few tools, we couldn't understand

The group learned much and had a marvellous time
Since Glasnost - I'm not sure what we'd find.

Christina B Cox

THOUGHTS

Is this your dream or are you part of someone's dream
Are you a figment of my imagination
Or am I a figment of your imagination?
Is this reality or is it fantasy?
Whose fantasy, yours or mine?
Where do we belong?

Does our body control our minds
Or does our mind control our bodies?
Are we programmed by one controller
Or do we control our own mind?

If dreams were thoughts
And thoughts were dreams
Who says that right is wrong?
Who says that wrong is right?
Who made the rules, are they right?
If they are right then who told them?
Where on earth do we belong?

Carol Williams

Cousins From America

What an E-mail surprise. A trip has been planned.
You are coming to visit from your far-off land.
Not long to go, the house is a mess!
Decorating to do, and I need a new dress.
'Don't worry,' they say. 'Mum, the house looks all right . . .'
Didn't they see the cobweb that appeared overnight?
Tidy the garden, stock up with food.
Place all the pictures where they are best viewed.
Such excitement you've caused! Hope our letters convey
How we have looked forward to you arriving today.
Have a safe journey. We'll watch the plane land.
Lots of hugs and kisses, and shaking of hands.
How the time flies! So much we have done.
Visited friends, reminisced in the sun.
The cases are packed, to the airport we go.
We are all getting older and we all know,
This could be the last of our meeting. Oh dear!
Perhaps I might manage a visit next year.
Long hugs, tear-filled eyes. Holding of hands.
It's time to go. There your plane stands.
'We'll write, we promise.' wiping each eye.
A last touch, a wave and a quiet 'Goodbye.'

Joy Cooke

If You Were Really . . .

If you were really happy just counting out the days . . .
If you were really waiting by sunny, windswept bays . . .
If you were really happy about the dreams I used to say . . .
If you really wanted something, just don't take me now away . . .
If you really wanted something that I could not e'r provide . . .
If you really wanted something that I would have stood there,
and just cried . . .
If you really wanted me to say that I will always be . . .
If everyone should whisper how much they all love thee . . .
If something stood in ways that I could not ever see . . .
If things were going on around me, never let it be . . .
If I will always love you till the ever lasting days . . .
It will always be a somewhere where we met and held our gaze . . .
If you really wanted me to do so, I would have stayed away . . .
Though the loneliness is sorrow, and the heartbreak grows
day by day . . .
If you told me that you loved me, I would not have gone away . . .
If you were really wanting, I would have stayed and stayed.

Fiona E Pearce

First Impressions Of Provence

Warm light pervades over parasol pines
And cyprus spikes, tips slightly windbent
Terracotta roofs, apricot and cream walls
Reflect fields bursting wild flowers and butterflies
Cork oaks struggle through splintered rocks
Near perched villages next Esterelle foothills.

Patched, worked vineyards stitched in grapes
Winding streets of cobbled paths, eaves touching
Sewn together by lines of multicoloured washing
Ill-fitting gateways, their planks, corners eaten
Faded window shutters hanging, paintless,
Weather-beaten, sun-bleached, slatted.

The quiet cafes, stripe blinded, window-boxed in geranium
Trickle fountains of carp with silver darting scales
Mouthing the velvet still surface
Slowly glide the copper green and ochre slimy stones.

Tony Matts

WORLDS APART WITHIN

It's not an alien planet, just a spot upon our globe.
A piece of land made special from nature's rich abode.
Where happiness is everything and sadness frowned upon
A place of pure enjoyment, a jewel in the sun.

A kingdom of magic where the old become young
Filled with rides of fantasy, masters every one
They strike at the emotions, love, fear, hate are but a few
And hold you in their ecstasy, like any space-probe crew.

The spirit of adventure is held within this ring
Sailing on the river; charmed by bears who sing;
Climbing through the tree-tops; on board the Thunder's race;
Chasing that Brer Rabbit to find his laughing place.

Flying with Dumbo, Peter Pan and Mr Toad.
Facing ghouls and ghosts within their haunted abode
Sailing on a stern-wheeler a proud ship of the past
Exploring Sawyer's Island where crazy rocks turn fast

The future has conquered the blackness of space
And rockets return their payloads safely to base
An alien encounter is sure to take place
Where electro-magnetic transport is provided for the race.

Around the shore of a man-made gigantic lake
Lie factual portrayals of many of our nations
A chance for all to see the practice of co-operation
Forging bonds through their joint participation

These are Worlds within a World not places of retreat
They are what should be, a target for our World we entreat
No lies; no cheats; no politicians
Just love and happiness whoever we meet.

Terry Baldwin

THE EYES OF AN IBAN CHIEF

The eyes that looked down from this throne on stilts,
With a vigilance o'ersaw,
This tribe, this family of kith and kin,
These eyes that kept the law.

From childhood days of Mother's love,
Of tears, of joy, of fun,
Of games with sticks, and stones and bones,
On this island in the sun.

Of mothers and sisters with daily chores,
While children played around,
Of animals and birds with shrieks and calls,
A cacophony of sound.

From teenage years when skills were learned,
The kill, the word, the fight,
Of building Longhouse tall and proud,
Where rain fell every night.

From thoughts so clear of hunters proud,
Who guarded in the jungle,
Their tribal home, this piece of land,
Beneath the Heavens rumble.

With rice wine raised in knotted hand,
A toast for those to come,
A legacy, a treasure passed,
To this his eldest son.

The eyes grow dim but fill with pride,
When standing near at hand,
They come to rest upon the man,
Whose eyes will watch this band.

J C McKenzie

JAPAN

Scenes of splendour mix
with endless streams of platform
shoes and duffel coats.

Kathryn Seymour

SUNRISE

At dawn on that wonderful holiday,
We stood there, my husband and me.
In silence, his hand on my shoulder
As the sun rose up out of the sea.
We gazed to the distant horizon
Just a line between two shades of grey.
The world fresh and still and in waiting
For the glorious start of the day.
The first fragile tinges appeared in the sky
Of the palest most delicate pink
Which grew stronger and deeper as seconds passed by
Till at last it was there on the brink.
Upwards and onwards that great ball of fire
Slow and steady ascended to view
Casting silvery beautiful shimmering rays
As it climbed up on into the blue.
It travelled its course to the heavens.
Our spirits flew high with delight.
Touched by the heat of the luminous glow
And encircled in radiant light.

Susan Barnes

BLACKPOOL 2000

Once full of life, once elegant,
This town displays its peeling paint
And gaudy shop facades.
The rigid roller-coaster frames
Stand skeletal in the rain
With no one on the rides.

A Gypsy Rose will tell you all,
In among the candy stalls
And penny slot machines -
Which sate desire for gain:
But beggars ask in vain
For change from rich or mean.

The awesome tower, once built for glory,
Now tells quite a different story
Of jaded guest-house owners;
Of tawdry clubs now for the masses,
Hotels with dusty plastic roses,
Of faded guest-house parlours.

In Stanley Park, though, far from stress,
A coot, by lakeside, sits on nest
Entwined with string and dross;
While raven-black in yashmak veils,
Girls flutter round the face-paint stall,
Enjoying candyfloss.

As placid swans show off their plumes
Italian gardens burst in bloom
And squirrels dart unseen.
This beauty here, all innocent,
Survives amongst the decadent
And Blackpool is redeemed!

Irene Munro

THE TRAIN

With the trees rushing by,
and the cold wind in my eye,
I summon up a tear,
and then begin to cry.

The people I've left behind,
who are all loving and kind,
I close my eyes and I can hear,
in the future I will try to find.

Speeding away from what I know,
but out the window the time goes slow,
whistling in my head a tune,
it's come for my time to go.

When I get to somewhere I'll call,
you have helped me learn to fall,
I promise to come back soon,
forever I will love you all.

Jamie Barnes

Far And Away

Sitting here in my room
I sometimes think
I wish I was on holiday
Places like Hawaii or Australia

But the place I always
Think and dream
Of going is New York

I'd love to go there
With things to see
Like the Big Apple
And lots of shops to shop at

It would be really good fun
I could go to the beach
And play around
And the weather would be great.

S Esat

First Love

The first white love of my youth
Burns privately, quietly, neglected
In the corner of my mind.

From time to time,
I revisit and re-examine
Those honied days;
As one sits and sifts
Through old favourite photographs.

Sweet reflections
Make real-life seem so dull.
Suddenly, as in my youth,
You become a habit in my head.

Over and over, over and over again
I glimpse a heart-stopping, intoxicating
Exhilarating, speeding car journey.
A sultry summer's night,
Two heads inclined together
A deserted golf course
And those restless, heady hours
Of our final encounter.

Your ghost rekindled
Appears to me in a dream
I ask you:
'Why did you forsake me?'
The vision blurs.

You turn once more
As if to speak,
You smile a faded smile
But you,
Do not answer.

Deborah L Wilson

Down Under

Australia: in Sydney we saw birds with plumage bright
And heard their unfamiliar songs that drifted through the air.
We visited our cousin's home. They took us to the park
To see the bounding kangaroos and hold koala bears.

Inside Sydney aquarium there darted brilliant forms
Of every colour, many shapes and sizes. Sharks were seen
And tiny fish as they swam by so close that we could view
Their varied stripes and patterns, glinting in the liquid light.

We sailed around the harbour next and passed the opera house
That is so famous for its architectural design,
Then disembarked at Manley beach and walked along the sands
And everywhere was light and warm beneath the autumn sun.

We then flew off to New Zealand and with more cousins stayed.
They overlooked the bay of Islands - views unparalleled,
Surrounded by exotic blooms and different kinds of trees.
There was a beach below their home that we could reach with ease.

A cream boat trip around the Islands, blue and limpid sea,
As we progressed from isle to isle, at midday anchoring
At a deserted island lush and there we had a swim.
It was all quiet and so far away from traffic's roar.

Then off we went again by coach to view the many lakes
And to absorb the sights and sounds of mighty waterfalls
That thundered down from heights so great. The hidden mountain peaks
At times appeared as clouds sailed by, revealing caps of snow.

When visiting the geysers there we saw the boiling mud;
Were entertained by Maori songs and dances at a feast.
We flew up to Fox Glacier and walked upon the ice.
So many memories I hold of that exciting flight.

I loved the beauty of the open countryside - the peace.
The only traffic jams we met were flocks of passing sheep!

Anne Greenhow

My Favourite Place

Paris in the spring is a romantic thing
The Eiffel Tower there by the hour
Those crooked streets if they could speak
J'taime, J'taime, J'taime

Roma, Roma what are you like?
The Itis they argue, they like a good fight
Pisa it leans, how long will it hold
This city of passion to me you have sold

New York, New York is more upbeat
A Statue of Liberty that stands on her feet
A sky scraper high the folks are not slow
The Empire State Building, why don't you go

London, London are you like home?
Buckingham Palace, the Millennium Dome
Trafalgar Square the pigeons do dwell
My favourite place . . . I really can't tell

Fiona Ball

DELAYS

It was to be our fate
Our departure from Berlin was late
The collection of luggage from hotel room
So slow it filled us all with gloom
But Albert, our driver did his best
To make up time while we took our rest
We arrived at a new Polish border post
We'll soon be through, was the thought of most
But the border police made a careful check
Of passports and visas and so did wreck
Our hopes of reaching Warsaw early today
We sat on the coach filled with dismay
Folk from Canada and Oz need the police okay
So we can proceed without further delay
The border toilet although new and clean
Lacked any paper which seems to be mean
'You may go,' an officer eventually said
And without further ado off we sped
But only for a hundred metres or so
For customs' officers made our Aussie friend go
With them; his luggage to check at leisure
Four hours late, we could travel for pleasure
We arrived at Warsaw at a late hour
So Gary, tour director said nothing more can sour
Our trip, but he spoke all too soon
He learned that for some there was no room
And off to other hotels they were sent
It seemed for Gary trouble would not relent
Next day however all was forgiven
Touring Warsaw was just like heaven
And the weather too played its part
So now we are feeling in good heart

The delays which at first made us want to walk
Gave us opportunity for friendly talk
So Albert and Gary please don't despair
We all have confidence you'll get us there.

G T D Skelton

A Proper Holiday At Last

My last holiday was a pilgrimage,
Inspiring for its religious value.
Not an adventure, that's for sure,
In retrospect, rather a bore.

Now thirty-five years later,
I'm off to north east Yorkshire.
I've never been there before,
It will open my mind's door.

Our bus arrives at six o'clock,
Into the Talbot hotel, Malton,
Like a straggling group of sheep, we flock.
I long to escape to my own room,
Put my belongings in order and rest.
I've a feeling of curiosity and zest.

Off to Scarborough in the morning,
Donkeys, electric powered lifts and golden sand.
We go to York on Thursday,
I expect York Minster will be impressive and grand.

One day we saw the Yorkshire moors,
Heartbeat country - Aidensfield.
To this part of Yorkshire,
My heart does yield.

I stared in awe and surprise;
Could not believe my eyes,
When we drove through that special place.

For my York visit, I devised a scheme,
To see the city of my dreams.
I rode on an open top bus.
A guide related many interesting, historical facts.
Less walking, no hindrance, no fuss.

Linda Webster

Natural Beauty

Natural beauty is all around
A sight, a feeling, maybe a sound
Sun arising as day is dawning
The birdsong in the early morning
Fresh aroma of April showers
A garden full of pretty flowers
Bluebells along a wooden path
The night sky after dark
Warmth of a hot summer's day
A rainbow's bright colourful array
Raindrops falling on my face
Children's laughter in a school race
Cool, gushing mountain streams
Golden colours of autumn leaves
White wonderland of winter snow
Toes so cold but noses glow
A Christmas tree standing tall and proud
Yes - natural beauty is all around

Sheila Waller

The Apple Orchard

When I was ten, apples came from market barrows,
Weighed on black iron scales on a city street,
Brown paper-bagged home to parlour fruit bowl
And eaten, when invited, as a treat.

When I was eleven, I lived next to an orchard
And discovered one of God's perfect wonders,
Saw rosy-pink snowflake blossoms fall
Revealing cherry-size apples hidden in under!

An evacuee in the quiet English countryside,
I could pick fruit straight from the trees
By the bushel, apples, plums, pears,
Damsons, all loved by the birds and me!

In winter the gnarled old mossy boughs
Wrapped in snow looked wizen and bare,
But when spring arrived the tempting sweetness
Of myriad chiffon blossoms filled the air.

Knee deep in moist grassy fronds I'd wander
Beneath the heavily laden trees,
Watching the fruit grow firm and rounder,
'Dumpling' apples sure to please.

Shiny green Bramleys grew the biggest,
Ordained for succulent pies and crispy crumble,
Russets, Beauty of Bath, Cox's Pippins,
Finding our mouths before they tumbled.

Dumpier trees bore scraggy apples for cider,
'Scrumpy' farmers called it in Somerset,
Gathered and piled into a horse-drawn wagon,
Their fate a gigantic cider-press!

Apples squashed by the loadful,
Brown, aromatic liquid oozing into huge vats.
Nothing wasted, left-over mash fed to pigs,
I wondered 'Did they ever get drunk on that?'

In autumn as leaves shrivelled and fell
Prize apples were hand-picked for store
Providing delicious desserts for the winter,
Then next spring would bring some more.

Pat Heppel

Oberammergau

Snow-capped mountains proud and regal
Sweep down to the fields below
Houses stand festooned with flowers
This is Oberammergau

Shops display handmade wood carvings
Formed by experts in the craft
Frescoes grace the walls and buildings
Painted scenes depict the past

Death from plague had reached the area
In year sixteen thirty-three
Villagers begged God's compassion
And deliverance from disease

They were saved and made a covenant
To enact a Passion Play -
Each decade, from then, for ever
Vowed and acted to this day

In the play, a cast of hundreds
Fill the vast impressive stage
Village people are the actors
Each performance to amaze

So the people come in thousands
Keen to see the play unfold
Portraying the Saviour's suffering
Reverently and skilfully told

In this small bavarian village
I was there among the crowd
Thankful to have gained these memories
Set in Oberammergau

Sheila Wyatt

June In Argyll

Shining collage sweeps across my mind:
Green wooded slopes,
Seen through silver curtains of rain.
Impossible peaks,
First crayoned hills of childhood
Soar into mist,
Where eagles hang, like flying pennants

Hedged in swathes of pine or granite walls,
Yellow flags spring
Thick, in pockets of wet meadows.
Blue skies harry
Columns of low stratos clouds, grey,
Yet light riven,
As headstreams over clarified pebbles.

Blue expands, intensifies, electrifies,
Engulfing rain
Heralds the blazing sun, which arcs to earth
In molten gold of broom.
Intersecting all, waterfalls plunge,
Explode in rainbows,
Sing their interminable song.

Elinor Wilson

The Hunger Of The Heart

The hunger of the heart
Is wrapped in need,
In sleep my wildest dreams
Come alive.
I awake each morning
Knowing you are there, my soulmate,
Loving words but no demands
Do you dictate.
A life of bliss
Has come to this
As acorns small
Develop into a tree,
And so you stand so tall for me.
You're always there
When I'm in despair
But when you go away as you often do
And work calls and distant lands
My heart hungers for your call
Because our love is all.

Joan Hands

N'Djamena

The road is wide and dusty.
Mud-brick houses blink
  in the glaring, relentless sun.
Famished, bad-tempered, sandy dogs
  roam, scavenging intently.
Chickens scuttle and peck, while
  the ubiquitous goats spring and bleat,
    or nuzzle the black plastic bags
      which litter the ground.
The people! They live life fully,
  bustling, sweating, arguing, laughing,
    wide, welcoming grins shining
      in handsome, ebony faces.
The men sit drinking bili-bili,
  passing the common calabash
    from mouth to mouth, as they rest
      on wooden stools, talking volubly.
Mothers manage to sing
  as they pound the millet,
    endlessly, courageously.
The babies tied to their backs
  observe, wide-eyed, this busy world.
This is the present . . .
  Those small, unwitting citizens of Chad
    are its future!

Katharine Holmstrom

THE MISSION

Upside down in Aussie land,
Twelve thousand miles away,
A mission with a lady friend
From England in UK
Inside me this strange feeling,
I find so hard to quell.
A longing, mixed with passion,
With my heart, an arrow
  Embedded there to dwell.
I recall back on the journey,
Flying daylight into night,
Forward in the time-warp
And jetlag left from flight
My mission for my lady,
So sweet, refined and fair,
Her ailment making breathing hard
Through high altitude of air.
Enroute Bahrain to Sydney
From our UK Sussex shore,
Via the eastern patch of Orient
The port of Singapore.
Onward then to Brisbane,
From Sydney to the north
The events that caused our flight delay
To the finish of our course.
Brisbane then to Bundaberg,
From whence I set this scene,
Part mission now completed,
My weary lady can rest and dream.
Upside down in Aussie land,
My lady is by my side
As I pray all future hazards
Our good Lord may help to hide.

Ernest L Hannam

Ronnie's Life On The Oil Rig

(Tribute to my son-in-law)

Carol took Ronnie to Beccles in the early dawning
He had to be there at 5 o'clock in the morning
He got in the helicopter waiting for his flight
It passed over our house with lights on till out of sight
It circled round the sea dropping men off on different rigs to reach
Then back again to Beccles, flying over the sea and beach
It's hard work out there and the hours are very long
You have to have a medical because you need to be strong
You have to have a survival course as well in case you fall in the sea
It's not much of a life out there, it's lonely as can be
But there is no choice and you are glad of a job
When you are out of work and need to earn a few bob
We worry about him being all those miles away from the shore
And glad when we hear a call to say he will be home once more
But the few days he has ashore pass quickly away
When he gets another call to say 'Can you be ready today?'
Each time he goes out on a different rig, fresh faces to meet
But Ronnie doesn't mind as long as the food is good to eat
Let's hope the building trade will buck up once more
So Ronnie can come home at night and walk on the shore.
With our love, Dear Ronnie.

Olive Peck

May 1997 - Scottish Highlands

Scotland, oh Scotland, 'Will ye ner come back again?'
As we approach the Scottish highlands
Tired, after hours enroute
The scenery, was awe inspiring
Snow-capped mountains touch the sky
Fluffy cotton wool clouds, gently float by
Glen and valley rolled before us
Lochs of shimmering, shining water
It was breath-takingly gorgeous
'Tarbett Hotel' on 'Loch Lomand's' shore
Like a fairy castle, who could ask for more?
'Highland stags', majestically in grandeur stand
Golden eagle, on tree stump lands, Scottish scenery, rolls away
What a beautiful picture, to behold
In one's memory, to take away
A Scottish welcome warms your heart
The food is beautiful! We all take part
Oban, Luss, with its quaint cottages
Sterling's sturdy castles, historic past
Inverary jail, cells made to last
A trip to 'Loch Lomand' was pure delight
Sun on water, wildlife, swans and all
A Scottish piper, playing in the glen, a truly memorable trip
Scottish dancers in kilts, with swords
Delight the guests as evening falls
Warm your cockles, with a dram as
Sun sets on loch, glen and brae
A perfect end to another wonderful day
Scotland, oh Scotland, will ye ner come back again?
To be sure! As soon as we can.

Irene G Corbett

MEMORIES!

I remember the farm, where as a boy,
  I spent my leisure time;
The woods and fields, I roamed with joy,
  the trees I used to climb.

I remember the games we used to play,
  the tricks we used to do;
I smell the scent of the new mown hay,
  I hear the first cuckoo.

I remember the work we used to share,
  of taking the milk around;
Where is the fun that we found there,
  that cannot now be found.

I remember the days when it would rain,
  and in the house we stayed;
I still recall the old refrain
  of records that we played.

I remember the fights we used to have,
  when sticks and stones would fly,
But you were always tough and brave,
  I never saw you cry.

I remember all those things and more,
  no matter where I roam,
Come let us seek the joy of yore,
  come let us both go home.

R Hogg

The International Eisteddfod

In the green valley of the River Dee
A festival of music, song and dance
Is held for six days yearly in July
The small town of Llangollen to enhance.

A 'Festival of Friendship' it is called
It fills the whole town from the dawn till night
And people of all races, colours, creeds
In love of music, song and dance unite.

Twelve thousand entrants come from fifty lands
To play and sing and dance and mingle there
And lifelong friendships made in that fair town
Are toasted in the homes without a care.

The choirs, musicians and the dancers there
Compete to win the trophies for the best
Performances that gladden every heart
For they sing, play and dance with immense zest.

The Obernkirchen Children's Choir came
To sing 'The Happy Wanderer' with a will
And many of those children oft returned,
Their love of the Eisteddfod lasting still.

Walk through the town, you'll catch the sound of choirs
Who practise in the chapels and the halls,
Walk back at night and they are dancing still,
Their costumes splendid as those worn for balls.

Its motto 'Blessed is a world that sings
And gentle are its songs' is dear to all
Who wend their way to this well-loved event
To sing and dance and on each other call.
To spread goodwill through all the lands on Earth
Musicians gain where politicians fall.

Joyce M Turner

ECHOES OF AFRICA

Africa, Africa, Africa
Our beloved continent cries
Problems, troubles haunt the continent
This is the voice of the Africans

In Mozambique
Floods destroyed infrastructure
Outbreak of diseases haunt the nation
Roads and bridges are non-existent
Please help poor Mozambique

In Zimbabwe
We need investors
We want employment creators
Zimbabwe a country with resources
For those who need real investments

In South Africa
Thousands are dying weekly
We talk of AIDS daily
Orphans are increasing daily
We cry for God's mercy

In DRC
We talk of war
Peace agreements being breached
We cry for peace in Africa
Peace, peace in DRC

In Kenya
We talk of hunger and starvation
Enamating from prolonged drought
Food resources are scarce
We really need urgent help
This is the voice of Africa

Handsen Chikowore

John Muir Wood

In a wood near San Francisco Bay
I and some others walked one hot and sunny day
The giant Redwood so majestic and tall
Providing us with shade to keep us cool.
As we walked through to our delight
We saw a truly wondrous sight,
A beautiful doe and her fawn
They were a little timid, as you would expect
But they stood their ground
As we mere mortals tried hard not to make a sound
We moved on and let them be
Wild, beautiful and free.

Lesley Anne Stevenson

Taj Mahal

Love expressed in marble - such a cold extravagance -
only a Mogul emperor could conceive
grief on so sublime a scale, his sorrow set with precious stones
and carved, as though construction might achieve

some respite gleaned from beauty and purity of form
when reflecting the dead whiteness of the moon,
its purpose clear, implicit, echoed in each faultless line:
his final gift the world's most perfect tomb.

A building born in anguish, his lasting passion burns
when eastern moonlight throws itself across
a Persian dome whose symmetry can resurrect the past
and so describes the hollow ache of loss.

J M Harvey

SUBMISSIONS INVITED

SOMETHING FOR EVERYONE

POETRY NOW 2001 - Any subject, any style, any time.

WOMENSWORDS 2001 - Strictly women, have your say the female way!

STRONGWORDS 2001 - Warning! Age restriction, must be between 16-24, opinionated and have strong views. (Not for the faint-hearted)

All poems no longer than 30 lines.
Always welcome! No fee!
Cash Prizes to be won!

Mark your envelope (eg *Poetry Now) **2001***
Send to:
Forward Press Ltd
Remus House, Coltsfoot Drive,
Peterborough, PE2 9JX

OVER £10,000 POETRY PRIZES TO BE WON!

Judging will take place in October 2001